Success Strategies for Affiliate Marketing

By

Adenekan Lateefat

Dedication

This book is dedicated to Almighty God and to my family.

Table of content

Introduction

One of the best methods to make money online is through affiliate marketing. This is a fast, passive, highly scalable, and simple to set up way to make money.

There are no technical requirements, and if you pick the right products and target the proper market, you might quickly earn hundreds or even thousands of dollars.

However, let's take a brief step back. First, let's define affiliate marketing. How does it function? And what makes it so much more efficient than other online business income strategies?

Affiliate marketing basically entails promoting someone else's product in exchange for a commission. Then, you get paid for each sale you make, so all you have to do is introduce that product to a market that will find it appealing.

You will frequently discover that you get to keep 70% or more of the revenues when selling affiliate products like eBooks! You can make just as much money with the appropriate product as someone who produced it themselves.You will learn the advantages of affiliate marketing in this book, along with how to get going quickly and effectively so that you can start earning money. This might actually improve your life with wise product choice, a ready audience, and a tiny bit of luck.

If you already sell affiliate items, this book should equip you with the extra knowledge and strategies you need to take the business you run to the next level. This includes the equipment leading brands employ to market HUGE ticket items like MBA programmes and laptops with price tags of $5,000 or more.

Chapter 1

Why making money through affiliate marketing is the greatest option for beginners

Many people struggle to understand the notion of affiliate marketing. How can you sell something that you didn't make and make money?

How is it possible that making money online is so simple?

It can be summed up by saying that it is essentially sales. When you sell something, you are operating as a vendor and getting paid a commission. In that respect, you resemble the door-to-door salespeople that visit you to offer broadband. The distinction is that you aren't knocking on doors. Your door is the internet, and via this door, you have access to everyone on the earth. That immediately gives you a significant advantage, especially once you figure out how to attract customers to come to you.The commission structure will also alter significantly in this case, which is another difference. Regular salespeople often receive a tiny commission of between 5 and 10% of anything they sell. As previously said, affiliate marketing differs in that you will receive up to 70–80% of the sales. That's correct, you'll frequently make more money as an affiliate marketer than the product's maker!

Because you can start earning as though you were selling your own product without having to spend a lot of money creating anything from scratch, affiliate marketing is incredibly alluring.

Additionally, since you'll be selling an item that is already on the market, you can pick something that is currently doing well. There is always a chance that you may construct a product that no one wants when you make your own to sell. That becomes far less likely when you just market something that is very well-liked! The fact that affiliate marketing is so scalable is just another fantastic advantage. You can start making money from an affiliate product within hours of creating a single web page that promotes its benefits. What would prevent you from creating another page to market a different product in that scenario? and yet another page to market yet another item?

How to use affiliate marketing

So, shall we go on to something a

little more technical? Why would a creative ever be content to give up so much of their own revenues and how exactly does affiliate marketing operate?

Let's start by thinking about the kind of content you will be selling. Affiliate products are typically digital for many marketers.There are other additional alternatives, which we shall examine later in this book. But for now, we'll concentrate on that. That includes stuff like presentations, online courses, and eBooks. Digital goods are an excellent alternative for online sales right away because they have no overhead and no "COGs"(a word used in business that stands for "Cost Of Goods Sold"). It follows that the creator may choose to generate a profit and divide it with others rather than having to make any payments at all for each sale. Additionally, it means that they have never had to make a sizable upfront investment and that they are not responsible for delivery.

Therefore, the person who created this digital product most likely used Word or a camera to create it themselves, however it's also possible that they hired a third party. In any case, they will have created this ebook or course with the goal of making money off of it. The creator will thereafter have likely started selling said item from their website or from a random online portal. To urge people to buy from them and create their own passive income stream, they will work to attract as much visitors as they can to their website. However, a single person can only perform so much promotion until their resources run dry. At that point, a creator might begin seeking for affiliates with whom they can collaborate to promote their products.

As a result, the product manufacturer is prepared to pay affiliates like us 70% or more in order to encourage us to promote their goods. Additionally, they want to persuade us to promote their goods rather than those of other creators, for which affiliate programmes are available. Despite the fact that the creator would now only receive 30% of sales, this is still 30% more than they would have otherwise received if they wouldn't have quit.And that seller will be generating enormous profits and much more than they could on their own if they can entice thousands of people to their books with a horde of online marketers. In a nutshell, both parties benefit from this. The inventor encourages marketers to collaborate with them, and as a result, they gain a thousand more purchases. Affiliates get to market a product as their own and keep the majority of the sales revenue! They can earn the same amount of money from their own eBook or course without having to create one and take that significant risk.

In particular, "affiliate links"are used in this process, which in turn relies on cookies to function.

You will be given an affiliate link when you locate an affiliate product you want to market; you must use this link on your sales page and in your blog entries. A customer will be taken to another web page when they click on your affiliate link. In this case, a cookie that identifies them as coming from you will be saved on their machine. Now, whenever they make a purchase from that store, it will be noted that they are "one of yours"and the commission will be put to your account balance for you to withdraw at a later time. You just need to advertise the product and give the link. All there is to it is that!

Chapter 2

How to locate and market affiliate product

Okay, enough with the speculative language. How exactly do you begin and develop your affiliate marketing career?

So, you're going to need a product first. You must visit a website like Clickbank or Commission Junction in order to obtain this. JVZoo is an additional good one. You can browse a wide range of things here that are available through affiliate programmes. Simply go through and seek for the ones that catch your attention. You'll discover that you may view some details about the various products, so attempt to search for items that are selling for a fair price and providing a good commission. Some sites will let you see a rough number of sales, in which case you of course want to look for the items that are selling well. Once youve identified the product you would like to promote, you then need to contact the owner. If you are successful, theyll provide you with your link and youll be free to use that as you choose. Something else to keep in mind here though, is that many affiliate products will include marketing materials along with them.

Remember: if you are doing well, that means that the creator is doing well. They will frequently offer resources like emails, a sales page, banner ads, and other things because they have every incentive to see you successful.I definitely advise choosing a product that offers these kinds of advantages if you're someone who is brand-new to the field of marketing. By simply copying and pasting the resources you already have, you can start working nearly immediately in this method.

Then you should see that you are selling in similar quantities given that the product and the sales pitch are identical. There is no reason why it shouldn't function just as effectively.

This business approach is just a "copy and paste,"as I have stated. You are simply duplicating a strategy that someone else is already using to sell a product successfully while making sure that the money goes into your bank account.

Although selling eBooks on websites like JVZoo is a great

strategy to make sure you can keep the most money possible, it does have some drawbacks. Contrary to what some other marketers may claim, physical products continue to be the most common form of product sold online. And if you give it some serious thought, this makes sense. How many people do you know that purchase tangible products? Almost everyone, right? How many individuals do you know who would purchase an ebook, though? If it's not through Kindle, your grandmother might not be able to because she doesn't know how to utilize PDF files. The same goes for your pal who doesn't enjoy reading; they probably wouldn't both! You essentially have a significantly lesser share of the market as a result.

What steps do we take to offer

physical products as affiliate marketers? The most well-liked choice is to sign up as an Amazon Associate.

A lot of marketers are drawn to Amazon's associate programme, which is their take on an affiliate programme.

You'll probably discover that the majority of information about affiliate marketing focuses on selling digital products through sites like JVZoo, ClickBank, and Commission Junction.Things are different on Amazon.com. Since Amazon already splits the profits with the producer and must cover storage, shipping, and postage costs, they are typically unable to offer you discounts of more than 4% or, at most, 8%.This implies that in order to make a decent profit, you'll need to sell a lot more goods at much higher prices.

Do you need to disregard Amazon Associates as a result, though? In no way.

To begin with, selling physical products is frequently far more lucrative than selling digital goods. If you had to choose between something you could hold in your hands and show to people and something you had to read on a computer screen, which would you be more likely to spend a lot of money on?

Even better, Amazon is a trusted brand with a solid reputation. They can buy from them with only one click, thus they are far more inclined to do so!

There will almost always be something appropriate to go with an article because Amazon offers such a vast selection of things that you can sell.

Last but not least, even if a user hits on your URL but then purchases anything else from Amazon, you will still get paid! If someone were to purchase a new computer, for instance, and you were to receive 8% of that sale, you might possibly earn a sizable sum of money.

As long as you directed the customer to Amazon in the first place, you would still receive that fee even if you didn't actively promote the products.

the best course of action? Use both affiliate marketing strategies! But make sure to include Amazon in the calculation or you'll lose out. You'll learn how to market Amazon products a little bit differently in later chapters to make the most of them. (Note: One restriction of Amazon Associates is that it is impossible to get money if you don't reside in the same nation. In other words, you must direct your consumers to Amazon UK if you are headquartered in the UK. Amazon.com sales are still possible, but you will only be able to swap them for vouchers.)

Alternative strategies for selling physical products

Of course, there are other options for selling actual products besides Amazon.com. There are several manufacturers who will offer affiliate programmes directly to marketers, in addition to the countless actual storefronts that exist.If you take the effort to search for alternative products, you might discover something that is far more closely related to the subject of your website (and hence more likely to sell).Try searching on Google with your topic followed by "affiliate programme"to uncover these affiliate programmes. Online, there are several lists of the top affiliate programmes in every business. Another option is to direct a manufacturer or seller that doesnt offer an affiliate program... and then to ask them if they would consider creating one for you. If you manage to do this successfully, you can strike up an exclusive deal and potentially get a large commission too. Of course, for this to work, you need to be able to demonstrate that you have the reach and the influence to make it worth their while.

Selling services

Selling a service or an SAS (Software As A Service) is an additional choice.

The most profitable choice may be this one! Because many services will give you a recurring commission, this is possible. Let's imagine you are successful in persuading someone to register with a gaming website. Some online casinos give commission on every win made by that customer throughout their whole relationship with the company! In the same way, if you can persuadr another recurring service, you will frequently discover that you are offered a commission that is paid to you each month that they stay with that provider.Of course, there may just be a modest commission at first. but over time, it might add up to a significant amount of time. you might have hundreds or even thousands of conversions in a few years, which would then generate ongoing revenue even if your website were to shut down!

Chapter 3

How to intelligently select affiliate products

Affiliate marketing is really easy to use and effective, but it is not fully foolproof. That is to say, you might not experience the kind of rapid success you were expecting if you pick the wrong product or promote it improperly.The appropriate product selection will then be crucial to your success. What you should know is as follows.

What to avoid selling

The majority of consumers load up their preferred affiliate network (ClickBank, JVZoo, Earnersflex) before searching for the products that have the highest sales and the highest commission.This is a smart choice because the statistics show that other people are making a lot of money, which means that you should be able to as well. Actually, their business strategy is one that you can 'copy and paste'!However, if that's all you're doing, you're doing it wrong. The top 99% of the products will all be focused on the same exact things: generating income online, dating, or exercising. If you start pushing one of those books, you'll be up against everyone else selling it and everyone else selling books that are comparable to it. Most internet users who have been using it for more than a day have become tired of being pitched "make money from home"schemes.

Furthermore, they are the online niches with the highest levels of competition. It will be very difficult to rank first on Google for terms like "Make Money Online eBook"or "Build Muscle"if you don't already have a very popular website or mailing list. You're putting yourself in a bad position.

Alternative strategies

Consider choosing something in a more specific niche as an alternative. Let's imagine you come across an eBook that is targeted at a certain field or profession, such as one that explains how to become a successful flower arranger. Although the audience is fewer and it seems less thrilling, your product is now distinctive.

Additionally, by commenting on a few flower blogs, you can quickly connect with those flower arrangers. Additionally, it will be much simpler for you to push your sales page to the top of Google for "flower arranging eBook."Additionally, it has a distinct USP that makes it simple to sell.Even better, though, is to consider your current marketing channels. What connections are available to you? Where are the most individuals to be found? What do those people find appealing?

Before choosing a product, consider how you'll sell it and how you'll get in front of your target market. That is the formula for success, and it is a tactic you can use repeatedly.

It makes sense for you to purchase a product that will appeal to your audience if your website is already popular and has a large following.

Numerous products

Also keep in mind that you have the choice of offering numerous things. Another significant benefit of selling digital products is the ability to easily add or remove items from your website without having to spend hours writing and preparing content. Multiple product selling has benefits and drawbacks. If you have a large website and use soft-sale strategies (see the next chapter), selling numerous things is wonderful. This enables you to provide a variety of rates for various customer kinds.

That being said, concentrating on a single product at a time will enable you to generate more buzz and enthusiasm about that product in particular and to develop a more streamlined website that sends all visitors to a single page: the buy page.

Selecting physical products
The approach for selecting physical

products is a little different. Picking items that are pertinent to your content and the average reader of your website should be your method once more. At the same time, they must be high-quality things that meet actual needs.The good news is that there is no need to risk a large initial investment by purchasing numerous things in bulk. You won't be confronted with a scenario where you have a warehouse stuffed with fidget spinners!

In other words, you can go with the flow and generally try everything to see what sticks.In order to appeal to all types of customers, I do advise you to offer a variety of products at various pricing ranges. However, keep in mind that you earn money on any purchases made once a visitor visits Amazon. That means that selling that particular item shouldn't be the top focus; rather, getting them to click the link and visit the page should! Create your website and find a web host. Create a new page and add your affiliate link and the sales page copy you received to it. Now that everything is set up, you can start selling and making money! In the chapter after this one, we'll examine the following action.

Chapter 4

Creating a following and promoting the products

Building an audience first is the secret to success when it comes to marketing affiliate products. This is the "catch"(in so far as there is one), as it implies that in order to generate the greatest amount of revenue, you must actually put in some effort and labour.The good news is that if you pick a subject that interests you, you will essentially be paid well for doing something you like.

However, you must first develop the following and earn their trust as an influencer in order to reach this position.

Exist any additional channels for

affiliate product sales? Yes, without a doubt. And in this chapter, we'll look into those as well. However, I still strongly urge you to create that audience and make sure that people are enthusiastic about your company.

How to build a successful brand

Naturally, it's difficult to acquire this kind of influence. It takes a lot of time and a sincere effort to consistently offer genuine value for people to the point where they will buy items just because you promote them.Creating a website and a significant social media presence is the first step towards doing this. Don't try to sell straight away; instead, take your time earning their trust and loyalty by continually giving top-notch content.What's most significant?

Possess a strong, distinct brand with a clear goal statement and a well-defined "buyer persona."(The buyer persona represents a picture of your "ideal customer.")

The biggest error is trying to build a website that appeals to as many people as possible in a very general way. This can be a bad tactic, just like the digital goods you initially purchase. The reason for this is that when you aim really high, you inevitably end up with a bland and uninspiringbrand.A "fitness"website, for example, is too general and overused to be well-liked. Competing with the entire internet is what it entails. How do you differentiate yourself in such a crowded market?. Instead, think about creating a website about fitness for people over 40. Consider Paleo Fitness instead. also CrossFit.

or exercise outdoors. or Extreme Bodybuilding. All of these alternatives have a much more distinct intended audience, a much more distinct mission statement, and a much more captivating hook. Each will appeal to fewer individuals, but those they do will be FAR more likely to engage and be thrilled that there is something available just for them.

The brand should then emerge from this distinct and sincere objective. That implies that a person should be able to tell right away whether they like your logo or the layout of your website just by looking at it. Your brand should clearly state who it is for and what it stands for, and your content should support that message.The dedicated bodybuilding website will likely be red and black with several dark photographs of very muscular men and articles about "boosting testosterone with compound lifts."

The paleo fitness website, meanwhile, will probably be green and white with pictures of people running outside in the great outdoors. All of this goes from here EVERYTHING should be consistent with this picture, including your advertising and social media posts.Then, ideally, when you select your affiliate product, it should speak to that same market. And you will promote it in that way and sell it using that selling point.The fact that you offer fresh, original content that reflects genuine expertise is ALSO essential.

Here's a surprise: you will NEVER sell the affiliate product if you hire a writer who is unfamiliar with the subject. Why?

Considering that the paid writer's only option is to investigate the subject and rehash it in their own words.Because they won't be familiar enough with the subject to recognise when something is inaccurate or out of date, none of the content will be fresh or informative.

Find a writer who is genuinely passionate about the subject or write it yourself. Why? Since they'll then have something BRAND NEW and fascinating to say!

Be brave. Be distinctive. Be enthusiastic. then pick a product that appeals to that same market.

Have no time for that? Don't worry; the options that are available to you are stated here.

Inserting your link

Selling as an affiliate marketer is

quite simple. You are given one link to promote a product, and from anyplace you position that link, you can get income.

The challenge then becomes, where do you place it?

Although this is one possibility, the majority of us will position our link on a landing page or sales page. We'll examine that process in this section, along with a few more possibilities.

Establishing a sales page

A website's sales page is a page created expressly with the intention of closing a deal. This implies that it won't offer any further content (i.e., articles), links, or even advertisements. Anything that can risk diverting attention from the product you're selling shouldn't be present here.A sales page will typically have a very long and narrow layout, which will encourage users to stay scrolling and spend more time reading what you have to offer. They will feel like a waste of time if they leave without making a purchase, which makes it much tougher for them to do so! The writing is most crucial, though. If you craft your sales speech effectively, you may convert this captive audience into eager customers.A very effective tool that can make you a marketing Jedi is persuasive writing. You're not looking for these drones, are you?

The bottom line is that you will be far more successful at making sales, gaining subscribers to your list, and generally completing whatever objective you set if you know how to use words to persuade an audience.

What is the process for acquiring this superpower? Here are some ideas to consider:

Attract attention: People don't have time to read through lengthy passages of material. You must first convince your audience to read what you have to say if you want to persuade them. Why do you do this? One strategy is to start off strong.

Another strategy is to draw viewers in with a narrative format. The latter is very effective because it is obviously quite difficult for us to stop reading a novel before the end! People aren't always going to trust you since they haven't met you and they know you're just trying to sell them something. So use facts and data to your advantage. Let the numbers do the talking instead. Your argument will become more convincing the more facts you can cite and experts you can cite.

Anticipate:Try to foresee the problems that your readers will have so that you can immediately address them. You may, for instance, note that there are "many amazing sounding offers online,"but you should emphasize that this isn't "just another scam."

Risk can be reduced since 'loss aversion' is a fundamental human tendency. This indicates that they are more eager to keep what they already have than to get anything new. Then, you must eliminate all risk factors by providing money-back guarantees and risk-free trials. Understanding the value proposition is crucial. The promise that your product can transform your readers' life is what gives it its emotional significance. You should be aware that you're not actually selling an eBook on fitness, for instance, if you're selling one.

The feeling of having endless energy, six-pack abs, and tonnes of confidence is what you're actually selling. You must concentrate on that! Try to make the reader feel something by speaking from the heart, ideally excitement for purchasing your product.Keep in mind that many digital items will include pre-made sales pages similar to this, so you can just copy the script wholesale and put it on your own page.Now that you have your sales page, all you need to do to start getting conversions is point your audience there. Emails and social media product promotion can be used to accomplish this. You can even place product advertisements on your website's sidebar and in other places.

Building store

You can create a store to sell them from if you are selling several affiliate products, which is also a very good technique. This means that, like you do at an e-commerce site, you'll be highlighting and pushing goods that are pertinent to your brand. The only significant difference is that the customer will now be directed to an external page when they click on your item.It's easy to accomplish this; for instance, you might use WooCommerce, a WordPress-compatible e-commerce plugin. You'll be able to do this to create a store from your website where visitors can browse products. When someone clicks on an item, they will be directed to the new page using your referral link because it supports affiliate content.

More ways to sell

However, what about including links directly into the text of your articles? Although very few affiliates use this opportunity, it's a fantastic way to monetize a website or blog. Write about any topic you're interested in, and then include an affiliate link in the body of the article. By doing this, you can quietly promote the product, and anyone who is interested in your material may click on it.

Similar to adding AdSense to your page, however you get to actively push visitors to click the link and earn a much higher income. Even admit that it makes you money if you want to!

In fact, it is against the law to mention that you are making money from those things in many regions of the world. Use a plugin to put a note to the bottom of each page on your website to make this simple, but don't forget to do it!

The top ten list is one of the greatest content formats for promoting affiliate items. If you work in the fitness sector, you could compile a list of the greatest home gym machines, and if you write about technology, you could share the most potent laptops now available.Whatever you want to do, this will work great for clicks and revenue and will also lend itself to rich snippets, which can significantly assist in making your content stand out on the search engine results pages (SERPs).

Similarly, there is nothing that prevents you from including an affiliate link in an email's body. This is an excellent method for getting in front of people directly in their inbox at a time when they could be open to your offers.EBooks can also contain affiliate links. You can include links to your PDF if you are selling or giving away a digital product. People who are reading this are probably really interested in your brand and will thus probably buy what you suggest. Since these are qualified leads, this is the ideal setting for trying to sell even higher ticket items.What if you could offer a digital product for $20 per unit and then earn a tonne more money from everyone who reads the book and takes your advice?

Another option is to include an affiliate link on a printed flyer or booklet. The ideal method to do this is to redirect to your affiliate link using a more memorable and straightforward URL. In this manner, you can market your goods in person!

These recommendations are intended to show that you don't always have to be aggressively pitching your product; instead, you can try the soft-sell by simply including the link, possibly with an image.

This is extremely effective for physical products, provided the button is well-designed and the product is directly tied to the information on the page. Simply incorporating buy links into your material might result in a lot of sales trickling in, and they all add up if you have a successful site with lots of viewers and plenty of content.

You just need to be inventive to use affiliate links in a variety of other ways.Try out new things and experiment to see what works best for you and your product. You might be surprised!

PPC Marketing and Other Forms of Promotion

But what if there isn't someone there to listen? What happens if you don't have the readers' respect as an influencer?

In this scenario, you will need to figure out how to drive people to your sales page. The good news is that PPC (Pay Per Click) platforms like Facebook and AdWords make it simple to do this.PPC refers to a model where you only pay when someone clicks on your advertisement. You determine your budget's upper and lower limits as well as your maximum "per click"expenditure. If you set your cost per click too low, your advertisement won't display when there are numerous competing advertisements from other companies in the same market. If you set it too high, you probably won't make any money.

You can target the audience for your Facebook advertising based on the data that users share on the social media platform. These consist of:

Age

Sex

Location

Hobbies and passions

Occupation

 Income range

others' interests plus more!

The goal of using AdWords to place adverts on Google is to take into account both the person's purpose and their interests (based on the "keywords"they are using in their search).

Because it indicates whether a user is researching or shopping, intent is a crucial factor in PPC.

When conducting research, individuals might type in "best computer games this year."If they want to purchase, they may type in the title of the video game or "cheap computer games."

Additionally, you can employ "negative keywords"to eliminate words and phrases (like "free download") that can imply a customer is uninterested in making a purchase and hence has the incorrect intent.PPC seeks to ensure that only those who are likely to make a purchase from you click on the link. This reduces your spending while raising your potential earnings. This means that the advertisements must be "targeted"to the right audience as precisely as possible, even to the point of scaring off potential customers with the appropriate content.

Of course, the link should drive users to a sales page in order to increase your revenue. The site's conversion rate is what you then need to concentrate on. In other words, if your landing page is nicely written, 1% of visitors may convert (i.e., 1% of visitors may make a purchase). The more you can afford to spend on advertising while still turning a profit, the higher this amount should be.

Direct selling through Facebook and other platforms

You can, of course, sell straight through those other sites as well. Nothing prevents you from posting an affiliate link to your Facebook group or your Instagram account (in your bio or once you are able to add the swipe up capability to stories). If you don't have the time or resources to design a website, this is a helpful technique to develop an interested audience.

Chapter 5

Powerful modern tools and strategies

Selling a variety of products, including physical, digital, and services, is significantly more effective because it combines the kinds of enormous sales you can achieve by cultivating a devoted following with the VOLUME that comes from moving a lot of physical products.And here's another thing to remember: Having such a wide range of affiliate products to sell on your website gives you the flexibility to include items that are "pie in the sky"sales. a case study? I once used an affiliate link to sell an MBA! This was done through EDx, an affiliate programme that has the potential to be extremely lucrative but also one that requires registration.The difficulty? juggling and managing all those various things! In order to access some of the most profitable affiliate programmes on the internet, the major, serious businesses will need solutions that ease this procedure.

Essential tools for updating affiliate marketing

Genius Link is among these instruments. You can join several different accounts using Genius (https://www.geni.us/), and then you can add their affiliate programmes. Since you can add accounts with all of the various local versions of Amazon, this works particularly well with Amazon.

You won't have to worry about losing customers because each link will then direct the user to the appropriate Amazon page based on their location. But you can also install a lot of other apps, like iTunes, BestBuy, and Barnes &Noble!

From this point, creating an Amazon link is as simple as copying the sales page's URL and entering it into a box.

Trackonomics (https://www.trackonomics.net) is a comparable choice. Similar to other tools, this one allows you to add things from a much bigger list of affiliates. That includes things like the EDx discussed above. Even better, Trackonomics enables you to look for products across a wide range of affiliate accounts and then select the one that generates the highest revenue.

In other words, if you are selling a

smartphone, you can now compare the commission you would receive if you sold it directly from the manufacturer versus if you sold it on Amazon. Compared to every alternative out there, not just Best Buy!

In order to determine which of your links is the most popular, to determine whether a link is down, or to determine how much money you have made over a specific period of time, both programmes also allow you to track clicks and transactions. The only drawback? Trackonomics has a MASSIVE $500 monthly fee. However, there is a free trial. Genius Link is free in the interim.

Extra Tools

These tools will enable you to increase your affiliate profits, but if you're looking to optimize your business strategy and sales funnel, there are also a tonne of other solutions available.For instance, using Google Analytics to monitor the effectiveness of your website and certain pages is practically required. You may check your position for various keywords, work on optimizing them, and then see which pages link to the sales page and which paths result in the highest commissions.

Similar to this, implementing technologies that enable A/B testing on your landing page can also assist you in optimizing it to the point where it significantly boosts conversions.

Conclusion

So there you have it: all the information you require to launch a highly successful affiliate marketing company. You decide whether to keep things straightforward or go for the moon, but I strongly advise you to follow the suggestions in this book and try selling actual goods that have wide appeal and high pricing in addition to the conventional digital eBooks and courses.

The traditional method of marketing affiliate products is straightforward:

- Get a link to a digital product you like.
- Establish a sales page.
- Link on the sales page
- Through promotion and traffic from your own website, direct

visitors to the sales page.

- Rinse and repeat after the item has finished selling.

To increase your income and create a more durable, long-term business strategy, I advise you to slightly modify this approach.

Here is the new approach:

- Make a website and attract a following that respects and values what you do.

- Create content that is genuinely original and passionate, and have a clear visual identity and goal statement.

- Create sales pages for a select high-ticket affiliate items and services, then "launch"them from your website using email blasts and teasers to build anticipation.

- Find the things that are the

most successful, and then use paid advertising to bring in additional visitors.

Meanwhile, through articles and websites that you promote using SEO, sell as many smaller digital products, Amazon physical products, and services as possible.Whatever you choose to do, you may now take advantage of making money while you sleep. The more you try new things, the more effective your sales strategy will be.

Know that, this information I give you, will not matter if you do not act on it. Taking action changes things.

Adenekan Lateefat.